I0461307

YOUR
PRESIDENT
KILLED
AMERICA

New World Order

Written by
Lewis Burt

All rights reserved. No portion of this book may be reproduced in any whole or part, stored in a retrieval system, or transmitted in any form by any means—electronic, mechanical, photocopy, recording, scanning, or other (except for brief quotations, critical review, or articles)—without the prior written permission of the publisher.

This book may be purchased in bulk for educational, business, or sales promotional use.

© 2022 by Words of Wisdom Publishing.
Published in Pittsburgh, PA.

Editor: Kya Publishing
Book Cover Design by Ashley Mae Pancho
Page Design: Osamudiamenabdul

ISBN (Paperback): 979-8-9857424-4-2
ISBN (Ebook): 979-8-9857424-5-9
Library of Congress Control Number (LCCN): 2022910917

Follow Lewis Burt on social media:

Twitter: @RealMrBurt
Instagram: @RealMrBurt
Facebook: @RealMrBurt

CONTENT

DEDICATION

THIS BOOK IS dedicated to everyone who has experienced, those who are currently experiencing, or those who will experience some form of adversity in their lifetime. Remember that you are resilient; your life has value and purpose regardless of what you may be experiencing at the moment. Please keep the faith, remain hopeful, and remember that you are loved.

ACKNOWLEDGMENTS

I would like to acknowledge the American people.

ABOUT ME

BORN AND RAISED in Pittsburgh, PA, Lewis believes in humanity, and could care less about politics. "*Your President Killed America: New World Order*" is a mirror into the heart and soul of Lewis: reflecting love, defeat, pain, maturity, and hope.

PREFACE

THIS BOOK IS not about politics. This book is about humanity, and the American people.

> **Proverbs 29:2** | *When the righteous are in authority, the people will rejoice; but when the wicked beareth rule, the people mourn.*

INTRODUCTION

I'LL NEVER FORGET the day when your President won the election. I remember waking up; CNN was already on my TV, but it was still muted. As I stared at the screen looking at your President's face, the color red seemed to be glowing around him. The red glowing around your President didn't look Republican. The red glowing around your President didn't feel like love. The red glowing around your president looked–and felt–demonic, and that just didn't sit right with my soul. As an American, I was hoping that my intuition was wrong about your President. As your President started to get comfortable in his seat at the White House, he made history in record-breaking time. I say this because your President didn't need a missile to kill our country: his cancerous character began to deteriorate the United States Of America the day he was elected President.

> **Psalms 135:15-28** | *The idols of nations are silver and gold, the work of human hands. They have mouths, but do not speak; they have ears, but do not hear, nor is there any breath in their mouths. Those who make them become like them.*

RED WHITE AND BLUE

RED, WHITE, AND BLUE used to run through my veins.

Now when I think about the flag, all I visualize is pain.

I used to feel a sense of peace when I would see the fifty stars.

Now when I think about the flag, all I visualize are scars.

Red, White, and Blue. It used to mean that we were free.

Now Red, White, and Blue are just colors I can see.

It means no unity. It doesn't mean that we are free.

Red, White, and Blue are just colors And that's three.

"America America," the home of the brave.

I've always had heart, but still felt like a slave.

I'm trapped in a country where everything is rigged.

Nothing has seemed to change, and it's been 400 years.

That's 400 years for my people and me.

Blacks were stolen from our land and were never treated equally.

Blacks are rarely treated fairly–most are forced to start from the bottom.

Racist cops slaughter Blacks on camera and your President forgets that they shot them.

I'll be damned if I let a racist white man kill me like Emmett.

Go to trail. Beat it. Then later admit it.

FROM ME TO YOU

DID YOU KNOW that your President pressured the Senate to enact the "nuclear option" to get his Supreme Court nominee confirmed? Nearly every other justice on the court had bipartisan support and crossed the 60-vote threshold at some point during their confirmation process, but many senators objected to your President's nominee. The nuclear option means Senate leaders can now confirm your President's ideologically-driven judges with a simple majority.

America's on a ventilator

Life left

93%

CPR for the Stars and Stripes

Treat people with dignity and respect, even if you don't know them.

> **Psalms 34:17-18** | *The righteous cry out, and the Lord hears them; He delivers them from all their troubles. The Lord is close to the broken-hearted and saves those who are crushed in spirit.*

THE WALL

WE FEEL TRAPPED because we can't get in.

I thought America was the place with a chance to win.

We had a chance to lose, and room to grow.

Now we're being deported from the country, so I guess we will never know.

Will never know what it's like to be free. Will never feel how it feels to be loved.

Our families have been divided by a wall, and now we can't feel their hugs.

How can we go on when there's a wall in our way?

Besides, your President doesn't want us here. So why should we stay?

The land of the free, and the home of the brave.

America, please don't bully us. Give us a chance to be saved!

Give us a chance to be loved, and a chance to be free.

Please beg your President not to build a wall around me.

FROM ME TO YOU

DID YOU KNOW that your President scared authorized immigrants away from accessing benefits and necessary health care for which they and their children are eligible? Not long after your President's administration took office, a draft executive order leaked, illustrating that the administration was looking to target even legal immigrants living in the United States. Among other provisions, the draft order would make lawful permanent residents—or green card holders—eligible for deportation if they used any type of means-tested benefit. The mere possibility of the order, as well as increased immigration enforcement, has had a chilling effect on communities across the nation.

America's on a ventilator

Life left

81%

CPR for the Stars and Stripes

Show empathy, and compassion for others.

> *2 Timothy 3:1-5 | But mark this: there will be terrible times in the last days. People will be lovers of themselves, lovers of money, boastful, proud, abusive, disobedient to their parents, ungrateful, unholy, without self-control, brutal, not lovers of the good, treacherous, rash, conceited lovers of God having a form of godliness but denying its power. Have nothing to do with such people.*

SHUTDOWN

I'M THE PUPPET MASTER, so I control the cops.

You don't need a chain for the door to America, because I control the locks.

If I don't get my way, I'll shut this country down... and everything will stop.

Screw your bills! I'm going to hold your pay, because I don't give a f**k.

The whole country is shut down, and that's the way I like it.

It's my way or the highway and when they give in, I get excited.

I'm the ruler of all. Nothing moves without me.

I can keep America shut down forever, because I'm king of this country.

I'm the ruler of all. Bow down to me.

I can shut America down when I please, because I'm king of this country.

FROM ME TO YOU

DID YOU KNOW that your President and his family continued to promote their private business interests at home and abroad while profiting off of the presidency? At a time when 75 percent of Americans already believed that corruption was widespread in government. Corruption–or even the appearance of corruption–diminishes trust in government, and increases cynicism toward democratic institutions. Your President's blatant disregard for ethics, rules, and constitutional prohibitions on presidential enrichment further undermine democratic norms and threaten our democracy, economy, and national security.

America's on a ventilator

Life left

78%

CPR for the Stars and Stripes

Do more for others than you do for yourself.

> ***Psalms 46:5*** *| God is within her, she will not fall; God will help her at break of day.*

WOMEN'S LIVES DON'T MATTER

WOMEN'S LIVES DON'T MATTER. That's what your President taught me.

Never consider them equal. Put them down, and just doubt them.

Men were born without women. That's how your President acts.

Your President disrespects women so fiercely. I'm sure that he lacks.

I believe your President lacks understanding of even his own being.

Without his own mother birthing him, he would not be breathing.

So why disrespect women, and boldly abuse your power?

Is it because you're heartless, and demonic? Is it because you're a coward?

In the seat that you sat in, you didn't inspire.

Instead, you chose to add flames to the fire.

The flames that would stop women from becoming their best.

You never wanted women to be considered, so you kept your foot on their necks.

What about the First Lady? Did you muffle her voice?

Did she want to say more for women's rights, but you gave her no choice?

I believe you silenced her. What woman wouldn't want to say more?

In the end, women's voices will be heard, and equality will be restored.

FROM ME TO YOU

DID YOU KNOW that your President reinstated the Global Gag Rule? One of your President's first actions as President was to reinstate the Global Gag Rule, which prevents recipients of U.S. foreign aid from offering any information, referrals, services, or advocacy regarding abortion care (even if they do with separate funding sources). The Global Gag Rule will lead to more maternal deaths, more unintended pregnancies, and higher rates of unsafe abortions.

America's on a ventilator

Life left

71%

CPR for the Stars and Stripes

Stand for something, or fall for anything!

> **Matthew 24:7-14** | *Nation will rise against nation, and kingdom against kingdom. There will be famines and earthquakes in various places. All these are the beginning of birth pains.*

Nation vs Nation

MANIPULATION FROM SATAN started an earthquake in our nation.

The Devil knew his time would come. He lurked, and showed his patience.

The Devil set a trap that was baited. The Devil hoped you would take it.

If you voted for the Devil, now you must embrace it.

Nation vs Nation. COVID-19 is on the rise.

Your President doesn't care about us dying, because he's the Devil in disguise.

The Devil only lies. I hope you're not surprised.

America will never be the same again until the end of times.

Don't stare him in the eyes! Don't let him brand you with his sign!

America, Satan is here, trying to rise.

It's up to you to choose, internally, to live or to die.

FROM ME TO YOU

DID YOU KNOW that your President ripped off American taxpayers and avoided fixing the federal coal leasing program? Your President's administration moved to preserve a loophole (that the Obama administration closed) that allows coal companies to rip off taxpayers by allowing them to sell coal (mined on federal lands) to their own subsidiaries at artificially low prices, and to shirk royalty payments and responsibilities.

America's on a ventilator
Life left
67%
CPR for the Stars and Stripes

Pray early, and often.

> *I Peter 2:19-20* | *For whenever anyone bears the pain of unjust suffering because of the consciousness of God, that is grace. But what credit is there if you are patient when beaten for doing wrong? But if you are patient when you suffer for doing good, this is grace before God.*

America's Great Again

AMERICA WAS GREAT when Blacks were forced to sit at the back of the bus.

America was great when we shared separate fountains because Whites didn't want to drink with us.

When women couldn't vote, we had them by the throat.

America was great, and it gave everybody hope.

Everything was split. Even where you sit.

America has always been segregated, and that history still exists.

Blacks were chained up on a ship. Now we coexist.

The White man brought Blacks here unwillingly. How great can it get?

For the White man, sky's the limit! For the Black man: they try to set a limit.

America is the White man's game. The Black man is just stuck in it.

Free us from these chains! Free us from this pain!

Don't try to ever erase our history by stating that this place can be great again!

FROM ME TO YOU

DID YOU KNOW that your President supported economic policies that are detrimental to communities of color? Many of the budget cuts proposed by your President would cut key social service programs. For example, 41 percent of the 9 million women, infants, and children (or WIC) recipients are people of color. The budget also eliminates the Minority Business Development Agency, which promotes business development for people of color–the fastest growing segment of the population.

America's on a ventilator

Life left

63%

CPR for the Stars and Stripes

Don't wait for change to come! Become the change!

> **Romans 8:18** | *Consider that our present sufferings are not compared with the glory that will be revealed in us.*

I CAN'T BREATHE

IN AMERICA I have no respect. It's like my head is under water, and a knee is on my neck.

I can't breathe!

In my neighborhood, all my friends are dying young. The killings have been consistent. Today teenagers own guns.

I can't breathe!

Police traffic stop. Both my hands are on the wheel. Do I have a better chance of running, or sitting still and getting killed?

I can't breathe!

My brothers died on the pavement. The police arrived on the scene and handcuffed me, and wanted a statement.

I can't breathe!

Unemployment is on the rise. Small businesses are closing. How long will we survive?

I can't breathe!

Ventilation system is running low.COVID-19 is on the rise. The death total will grow.

I can't breathe!

Will my vote count? Your President says it doesn't, because he got cheated...so it's out.

I can't breathe!

This country's feeling divided. Racism is at an all time high;
I pray that we survive it.

I can't breathe!

He's screaming for his mother saying, "I can't breathe."
He was thinking about his mother when he couldn't breathe.

I can't breathe!

FROM ME TO YOU

DID YOU KNOW that your President trampled on the religious liberty of Muslims with his attempts at unconstitutional travel bans? Your President's executive action on refugees aimed to prohibit travel to the United States for nationals of Muslim-majority nations, and fundamentally reshape the admissions program to prioritize the claims of Christians. Your President's actions have alienated the Muslim communities not only within the United States, but also around the world, damaging critical relationships with National Security Allies.

America's on a ventilator

Life left

50%

CPR for the Stars and Stripes

Please cease the war between #Red and #Blue! Choose humanity over politics!

> *James 2:8-9* | *If you really fulfill the royal law according to the scripture, "you shall love your neighbor as yourself," you do well. But if you show partially, you commit sin, and are convicted by the law of transgressors.*

WHITE POWER

WHITE SUPREMACY is everywhere.

It's hidden in the hearts of some teachers, and in the hearts of some cops.

If they're teaching racism, and not protecting us because of the color of our skin, will it ever stop?

What if it was rooted at the top?

What if your President was a racist demon?

That's a scary thought.

It would feel like a horror novel. We're all stuck in Salem's lot.

Your President's ingredients for disaster would probably be: hidden racism, and extreme manipulation, and then he would put them in a pot.

When your President finally opens the lid, the United States of America will be filled with steam and smoke.

Evil will overpower our democracy. There will be no more hope.

There will be no more hope for you. There will be no more hope for me.

Just like the beginning of times, though, there will still be hope for thee.

FROM ME TO YOU

DID YOU KNOW that your President undermined the legitimacy of the court system? As a candidate and also as your President. Your President attacked judges' rulings he did not like, and he undermined the legitimacy of these courts. Your President called a judge (who ruled against his discriminatory Muslim ban) a "so-called judge." During the campaign, your President said that a Mexican-American judge could not be impartial in a lawsuit against him, due to his ethnicity. These attacks on the third branch of government undermine the founder's separation of powers, as well as the very rule of law.

America's on a ventilator

Life left

44%

CPR for the Stars and Stripes

Choose love over hate!

> *2 Corinthians 11:13-14* | *For such people are false apostles, deceitful workers, masquerading as apostles of Christ. And no wonder, Satan himself masquerades as an angel of light.*

FALSE PREACHING

BELIEVE WHAT I SAY. Everything will be OK.

I would never lie to you, because I'm the President of the United States.

COVID-19 is not our problem. It will only spread in China.

Coronavirus will disappear very, very soon. Just give it a little time.

The vaccine will be here shortly. COVID-19 will go away.

Then everything will be very, very great again in the U.S.A.

Americans will be saved. The death total won't rise.

Just inject yourselves with disinfectant, and you'll have a chance to survive.

Come out and protest at my rallies so I can fill you with my lies.

Please don't wear a mask, because then this country will survive.

The Devil only lies. I hope you're not surprised.

Pay attention to the signs. It's the end of times.

The Devil is a lie. I hope you're not surprised.

Pay attention to the signs. It's the end of times.

FROM ME TO YOU

DID YOU KNOW that your President failed to help students when a critical resource for financial aid and loan payment was shut down?

In March of 2017, with no advance warning, the IRS and the U.S. Department of Education disabled a key web-based tool that helped millions of students.

America's on a ventilator

Life left

30%

CPR for the Stars and Stripes

Stop Asian hate!

> ***James 1:12*** *| Blessed is the one who perseveres under trial because, having stood the test, that person will receive the crown of life that the Lord has promised to those who love him.*

EMPATHY

I HAVE AN ICED TEA, and a bag of Skittles.

I'm standing in the middle of the street with my hoodie on, trying to solve this riddle.

Why are Blacks treated so little? Do Black lives really matter?

Every year, I lose count of cops killing Blacks on camera.

I'm starting to lose my stamina. I'm tired of this place.

In America I'm always considered last, even when I'm first in the race.

I know I'm a citizen of America, but still, I've never felt free here.

The gates of hell are covered with this country's flag, and I don't want to be here.

I'd rather kneel on my knee, but not to disrespect the flag.

I'm kneeling because I'm tired...but they don't understand.

They don't understand that it's time for us to react.

Why? Because for over 400 years in America, it's been hard being Black.

FROM ME TO YOU

DID YOU KNOW that your President proposed deep cuts to programs that help make college more accessible and affordable for low-income students and students of color? Your President's proposal summed up to more than 5 billion dollars in cuts to valuable programs– including the Pell Grant Program and the Work Study Program–that provide needed funds to help low-income people afford the rising cost of college. The cuts also target important college access programs (including TRIO and Gear Up) that provide support such as tutoring, mentoring, and research opportunities to low-income and first generation students.

America's on a ventilator

Life left

21%

CPR for the Stars and Stripes

Educate our youth on America's history with racism and segregation. Help to reverse the cycle.

> *Deuteronomy 28:68* | *Then the Lord will send you back to Egypt in ships, to a destination I promised you would never see again. There you will offer to sell yourselves to your enemies as slaves, but no one will buy you.*

OPEN WOUND

I WAS CHAINED up on a ship, but I made it off that ship.

I was also beaten with a whip, but I'm still just as strong as I was when I came off that ship.

Cotton's being picked and I don't make a cent, but I'm still just as strong as I was when I came off that ship.

A cop's knee is on my neck and I can't breathe a bit, but I'm still just as strong as I was when I came off that ship.

I'm screaming for my mother, with my last breath on my lips, but I'm still just as strong as I was when I came off that ship.

Will you remember this? Your President seems to forget that I'll always be as strong as I was before I was brought on that ship.

FROM ME TO YOU

DID YOU KNOW that your President turned a blind eye to illegal anti-transgender discrimination in schools? Your President's administration revoked Title IX guidance (issued by the Department of Education) clarifying schools, long-standing obligations under federal civil rights law, treat transgender students equally, and with dignity. Transgender students face pervasive harassment and discrimination in schools, impeding these students' ability to learn. Nearly 1 in 6 transgender K-12 students have been forced to leave school because of this harassment.

America's on a ventilator

Life left

17%

CPR for the Stars and Stripes

(The 8 Attitudes That Can Change America)

1.Honesty

2.Responsibility

3.Willingness

4.Open Mindedness

5.Humility

6.Caring

7.Objectivity

8.Gratitude

> ***James 3:16*** | *For where envy and self-seeking exist, confusion and every evil thing are there.*

PLEASE CONCEDE

THIS IS WORSE THAN 9/11, and sick Americans need help.

Our country is on its deathbed and your President is thinking about himself.

America can't breathe, and our lifeline is going flat.

All lives matter but your President doesn't seem to relate to that.

Conceding earlier (after defeat) could've saved millions of lives.

Just hand over the intelligence reports and push your pride to the side.

Do you even care that COVID-19 is on the rise?

Were you ever a real American? Was that another lie?

How could you sit in the White House with your feet kicked up and watch your country die?

The Devil is a lie, so again I'm not surprised.

I'm going to keep my faith in God until the end of times.

The Devil is a lie, so again I'm not surprised.

I'm going to keep my faith in God until the end of times.

FROM ME TO YOU

DID YOU KNOW that your President imperiled American voters with untrue claims about illegal voting? Your President's empty claims of widespread fraud undermine the integrity of our elections and lay the basis for voter suppression efforts that attack our constitutional right to participate in self-government. When government officials spread lies that call the legitimacy of our elections into question, people lose faith in the democratic process. Instead of responding to the clear and present dangers off foreign interference, and discriminatory efforts to keep some American citizens from casting their ballots, your President chose to spread baseless slander while calling for a witch-hunt against American voters.

America's on a ventilator

Life left

10%

CPR for the Stars and Stripes

#StandTogether or #FightAlone!

> **Revelation 13:1-8** | *And I stood upon the sand of the sea, and saw a beast rise up out of the sea, having seven heads and ten horns, and upon his horns ten crowns. And upon his heads, the name of blasphemy and the beast which I saw was like a leopard, and his feet were as feet of a bear, and his mouth as the mouth of a lion: and the dragon gave him his power, and his seat, and great authority. And I saw*

one of his heads as it were wounded to death; and his deadly wound was healed: and all the world wondered after the beast. And they worshiped the dragon which gave power unto the beast: and they worshiped the beast, saying, who is like unto the beast? Who is able to make war with him? And there was given unto him a mouth speaking great things and blasphemies; and power was given to him to continue forty and two months. And he opened his mouth in blasphemy against God, to blaspheme his name, and his tabernacle, and them that dwell in heaven. And it was given unto him to make war with the saints, and to overcome them: and power was given to him over all kinds, tongues, and nations. And all that dwell upon the earth shall worship him, whose names are not written in the book of life of the lamb slain from the foundation of the world. If any man has an ear, let him hear. He that leads into captivity: he that kills with the sword here is the patience and the faith of the saints. And I beheld another beast coming up out of the earth; and he had two horns like a lamb, and he spoke as a dragon. And he exercised all the power of the first beast before him, and caused the earth and them which dwell therein to worship the beast, whose deadly wound was healed. And he performed great wonders, so that he maketh fire come down from heaven on earth in the sight of men, and deceived them that dwell on the earth by the means of those miracles which he had power to do in the sight of the beast; saying to them that dwell on earth, that they should make a image to the beast, which had the wound by a sword, and did live. And he had power to give life unto the image of the beast, that the image of the beast should both speak, and cause that as many as would not worship the image of the beast should be killed. And he caused all, both small and great, rich and poor, free and bond, to receive a mark in their right hand, or in their foreheads: and that no man might buy or sell, unless he had the mark, or name of the beast, or the number of his name. Here is wisdom. Let him that has understanding count the number of the beast: for it is the number six hundred threescore and six.

ANTICHRIST

YOU BETTER GUARD your soul! The Devil is trying to take control.

Please guard your soul! The Devil is trying to take control.

Your character is being tested. Will you prevail?

Will you choose to burn in eternal fire when you enter the gates of hell?

Do you ignore the word of God? Do you stray from his signs?

If so, repent now, because this is the time.

This is the time when all your sins can be forgiven and washed away.

Don't wait another second. Give your life to God right now: today!

God wants us to all be happy and live peaceful.

That's what's offered in heaven, and nothing deceitful.

Hell on earth has always existed, but there's nothing to fear.

If your faith is strong, then you know that the Antichrist is near.

FROM ME TO YOU

DID YOU KNOW that your President undermined transparency and accountability by continuing to hide tax returns and by withholding White House visitor logs? Due to his refusal to release his tax returns, the full extent of your President's indebtedness and foreign entanglements remain unknown. As a result, Americans can not be sure that your President didn't provide favors and special treatment to his business partners or that foreign states and businesses were not leveraging influence over your President's administration and its decisions. It is impossible for your President to lead an effort to revise the tax code without Americans knowing how his proposals would line his own pockets. Changing the practice to stop disclosing White House visitor logs prevents the public from knowing who is accessing federal officials on a daily basis, and keeps special interest influence shrouded in secrecy.

America's on a ventilator

Life left

5%

CPR for the Stars and Stripes

Use your voice!

> **Proverbs 12:22** | *The Lord hates lying lips, but those who speak the truth are his joy.*

CHEATERS NEVER WIN

YOUR PRESIDENT stole the election from a woman who was capable, and he didn't know what to do with it.

Cheaters never win, so in the end...he looked stupid.

Your President was so ruthless.

Did he have a hidden pact with Russia? Is it possible that he loved Putin?

For your President, I was never rooting.

If you can hear me, I know the Devil is your father, and the flames sooth you.

I saw straight through you.

Make America great again meant the country segregated. I saw straight through you.

Blacks slain in the streets by police–now that's deep.

Your President is absent at the podium to speak.

Cheaters only care about themselves and their motives.

Cheaters don't care about America dying from COVID.

Cheaters don't care about you or your family.

Cheaters only truly do what's best for their family.

Cheaters never lose, so your vote doesn't count.

I guess that means even if you vote, that your vote doesn't count.

Can you beat a cheater? That's the question that I ask.

They're quick to steal their power, and they always seem to last.

Then I used my spiritual eyes, and I was aware that God was the ref.

When your President didn't concede, God called a tech.

Your President then went into hiding. Your President couldn't believe it. He was shocked.

I guess your President failed to realize that no matter what game we're playing, God controls the clock.

FROM ME TO YOU

DID YOU KNOW that your President attempted to bring back the War on Drugs? The outdated strategy was ineffective and caused long-term devastation to thousands of families. Attorney General Sessions is implementing a "tough on crime" approach that would increase federal prosecutions and long prison sentences even for low-level, nonviolent offenders. Even as your President's administration pushes outdated law-and-order policies, Democratic and Republican governors are making progress on sentencing reform, drug treatment, and alternatives to incarceration.

America's on a ventilator

Life left

1%

CPR for the Stars and Stripes

Become selfless!

> *Galatians 5:1* | *"It is for freedom that Christ has set us free. Stand firm, then, and do not let yourselves be burdened again by a yoke of slavery."*

EPILOGUE

FREEDOM IS A GIFT that should never be taken for granted. It is also a concept that means a lot of different things, depending on your perspective. The United States of America has always been labeled as a free country, but freedom is also something every individual experiences differently. The Bible contains many wise words on the subject of freedom, and it is a great resource for understanding the meaning of freedom and learning how to find it in your own life. For example, I used to look forward to reciting the Pledge of Allegiance to the flag as a kindergartner. Monday through Friday, the first thing we'd do is honor our country, or at least that's how I felt as a six-year-old. I used to feel so alive and free when I would say, "I pledge allegiance to the flag of the United States of America, and to the republic for which it stands: one nation under God, indivisible, with liberty and justice for all." Today when I see the flag that represents the United States of America, I feel pain, I feel betrayed, I feel trapped, I feel less-than, I feel dead. I feel like I'm entitled to my freedom of expression by choosing to kneel because of how the #Red #White and #Blue flag with the #Stars and #Stripes make me feel.

FROM ME TO YOU

DID YOU KNOW that your President proposed slashing funding for research to cure HIV/AIDS? Your President proposed devastating cuts to health research, including $6 billion in cuts to the National Institutes of Health in the budget, and a $50 million cut to the Centers for Disease Control and Preventions, HIV research and prevention programs. The administration has also pushed a $300 million cut to your President's Emergency Plan for AIDS relief (PEPFAR), an extraordinarily successful program that provides life saving treatment to 11.5 million people worldwide, with broad bipartisan support.

America is Dead

Life left

0%

CPR for the Stars and Stripes

America, always remember to lead by example. Remain positive and hopeful no matter what this country may be going through. Let your light shine through your character.

May God bless us all!

Also Available By Lewis Burt

Also Available By Lewis Burt

www.ingramcontent.com/pod-product-compliance
Lightning Source LLC
Chambersburg PA
CBHW060357130626
46553CB00003B/1268